MEDITATIONS WITH JULIAN of NORWICH

Introduction and versions by
BRENDAN DOYLE

Forewords by
PATRICIA VINJE
and
MATTHEW FOX

BEAR & COMPANY
P U B L I S H I N G
SANTA FE, NEW MEXICO

ISBN 0-939680-11-4

Library of Congress Card Number 82-73955

Copyright © 1983 by Bear & Company, Inc.

Bear & Company, Inc.
P.O. Drawer 2860
Santa Fe, NM 87504

Cover art & line illustrations—Sue Woodruff

10 9 8

Contents

FOREWORD: A Brief Biography of Julian of Norwich

Very little is known about the person who wrote these meditations and reflections, not even the author's name. According to the opening lines of the manuscripts that are available, she was a woman living in England during the fourteenth century. On May 13, 1373,[1] when she was thirty and a half years old, she reported seeing sixteen showings, or mystical visions. Quite soon after this event the young woman recorded the content of these revelations in a text entitled A Book of Showings.[2] Some fifteen to twenty years later, she produced an extended version of the same sixteen revelations. At some point in her life she became an anchoress and entered a cell attached to the Church of St. Julian at Norwich, in East Anglia. She took the name of the patron saint of her anchorhold according to the custom of anchorites and anchoresses. It is not known whether she embraced the anchoritic life-style before or after she wrote the later edition of the Book of Showings, but the civil records of Norwich indicate that the Lady Julian remained in the anchorhold at Norwich until her death sometime between 1416 and 1419 A.D.

This sparse biographical data provides some major clues about Dame Julian's spiritual and intellectual formation. She was born during the reign of Edward III shortly after England and France began to engage in a series of wars that would last one hundred years. It was a period of transition for ecclesial and governmental officials, although numerous history texts have described it as a period of decline and corruption. Both the Hundred Years War and the Black Death have been blamed for the so-called ecclesial and political breakdown, but the seeds of change had been developing for some time before these external crises shook England.

The impact of the shifting political and economic scene had a rather surprising influence on Julian's mystical writings. The very language of Julian's text was influenced by England's struggle to gain independence from France. English began to displace French as the official language of the people in the 1380s. Along with Geoffrey Chaucer and the other

English mystics, Julian initiated the process of writing in the Middle English tongue. The exercise of anglicizing her thoughts worked to Julian's advantage. She employed the colorful images that sprang from the wide assortment of English dialects. The flexibility of this new language, which she created as she went along, allowed her to express her message with a rhetoric and sentence structure that had never been used before her time. Her ingenious use of language continues to stand out because many of her linguistic devices and images have never been repeated. In the process of stretching and bending her words she developed a new way of talking about God. She expanded and clarified traditional church teaching on the Trinity, the role of Jesus in the Trinity, and the mystery of iniquity by means of her precise choice of vocabulary and her sensitivity to biblical and medieval imagery.

Besides the political upheaval going on at the time, a stream of natural disasters made their mark on the land and affected Julian's teaching. Most of the literature of this period reflects a spirit of pessimism arising from the suffering inflicted by a scarcity of food, the bubonic plague and unemployment. Julian's writings provided a welcome contrast to this contemporary strain of gloom. Like many of these authors, she touched on the themes of agony and grief, but she managed to present these miseries within a vision of a better life, not only in heaven, but in the foreseeable future as well. She urged her fellow believers to look beyond their uncomfortable predicaments and she encouraged them to cope with their misfortunes by paying attention to their neighbors and extending compassion to everyone else in need. Her deep faith and optimistic outlook soothed some of the discontent that was surfacing among her peers but the signs of malcontent were escalating. There was a growing sense of frustration with the taxation imposed by the government and a spirit of legalism within the established church. The preaching of mendicant friars had raised the intellectual status of the common folk and this precipitated irreversible rumblings in the lower echelons of the ecclesial and political structures. Equipped with a new sense of social consciousness, the laity now questioned the land-owning policies of the larger monasteries and chided the clerics for their lack of spiritual leadership. The preaching friars compensated for this lack of direction for a while, but eventually the alms bestowed on them by their enthusiastic listeners modified the simplicity which had been a major source of their spiritual charism.

The laity began to look to key lay people for their insights and spiritual enrichment. They were more satisfied with the advice and learning they received from mystical writers and members of the Beguines and the anchoritic movement.

Julian stressed the goodness of creation and emphasized the compassion and reverence that God has for each creature. Her emphasis on God's personal love for creatures unwittingly weakened the spirit of legalism which was providing a sense of security for the established leadership. Like her counterparts, Meister Eckhart, Johannus Tauler, and the author of the *Theologica Germanica* and *The Cloud of Unknowing*, Julian made slight references to the ceremonies of the church. She diligently strove to present a teaching that was orthodox and submissive to church approval, yet her appeal to the heart and conscience of the individual de-emphasized reliance on a sacerdotal religion.

Julian's understanding of God's fellowship with his creatures is at least partially due to her private revelations. It is not easy to calibrate the impact of the showings on her spiritual development, but traces of her mystical experience can be detected throughout her message. In a number of places in her text she explained how the revelations confirmed her previous religious training. She expressed a deep reverence toward everyone who would read her "lesson of love," a respect grounded in her understanding of God and the mystery of creation and redemption. This sense of honor was a natural result of the medieval notion of on-going creation. The doctrine of on-going creation viewed the initial act of creation as only one phase of the creative process; it emphasized how the Creator remains involved with his creatures' formation and development after he has made them. That is to say, it considered the reformation of creatures as a continuation of the first act of creation. Because of her upbringing within this theological tradition, Julian saw the redemptive love of God just flowing naturally out of his creative love, and textual evidence indicates that she perceived her mystical visions within this previous frame of reference.

Such a focus on the immensity of God's faithful and enduring love in no way diminishes the spiritual upheavals and social complications of this life. On the contrary, the tragedy of social sin and personal sin becomes more evident within the framework of Julian's creation-centered spirituality. The notion of God's compassion for sinners draws attention to the vast distinction between human and divine love and stresses the unnaturalness of humanity's aborted response to the invitation to love God with all one's might.

Despite her uncompromising convictions, Julian's anthropology and theology maintain an affirmative tone. This positive thrust is rooted in her understanding of creation as a self-revelation of the Creator. Her anthropology emerges from the creature's fundamental relationship with its maker. She emphasized the enduring nature of this primary relationship by noting that anyone who loves his creatures into being certainly intends to care for them and provide for their needs, whatever they may be.

Twentieth-century men and women who are seeking the same peace and security that their fourteenth-century counterparts desired can discover the same sense of affirmation and acceptance in the knowledge that God loves them, too, and desires to share a life of intimate communication with them. Julian's teaching promises today's men and women the opportunity to re-shape their perception of everyday life. It offers them the chance to lift their pain out of a problem-oriented context and to see how such difficulties are actually crucial components of the great mysteries of the creation, the cross and the resurrection.

Julian's meditations do not pretend to take away the pain of today's world, but they can inspire believers to rise up in the midst of the struggle and fix their eyes on God. They promote the virtues of self-acceptance and neighborly love and show how these qualities help creatures discover the face of God. This ability to recognize God in all things is crucial for creatures who are so prone to discouragement because they keep forgetting they are loved.

In addition to the personal benefits that can be gained from reading this book, it is my hope that the publication of these reflections can be a powerful antidote to the unfortunate disunity that still exists between the various religions of the world. Mysticism can be the source of unity among believers, but in order for this to be possible we have to get in touch with our own mystical traditions. As a means of preparing our world and our church to take the necessary steps toward unity, I want to invite each reader, as an individual, to step into the mystery of divine love as he or she reads the lines of this book, just as Julian entered into the mystery of on-going revelation when she recorded these words. Listen to her beckon all creatures, great and small, to look on the source from which they sprang and to return to the Creator the same compliment that was paid them when they were fashioned from the dust of the earth: Gaze on this creation and its maker and breathe forth the words "It is good!"

Patricia M. Vinje
Madison, Wisconsin
September 8, 1982

8

[1]Some manuscripts claim the revelations occurred on May 8 instead of May 13. This discrepancy is probably due to the partial illegibility or confusion of the Roman numerals viii and xiii. The Anglican Church celebrates the feast of Julian of Norwich on May 8 so a preference for this date must have held sway for a certain period of time. I use the critical edition of the Middle English text of the *Showings* which is edited by Edmund Colledge and James Walsh as my authority; see *A Book of Showings to the Anchoress Julian of Norwich*, Studies and Texts, Pontifical Institute of Mediaeval Studies Parts I and II (Toronto: Pontifical Institute of Mediaeval Studies, 1978).

[2]Other names for this manuscript are *A Revelation of Divine Love* or *The Revelations of Julian of Norwich*.

FOREWORD: Julian's Contribution to Spiritual Needs Today

Evelyn Underhill called Julian "the first English woman of Letters." This alone ought to make Julian of Norwich significant in Western history but in fact she has not been. While we are in possession of over fifty manuscripts of her contemporary, Walter Hilton, we have at the most five for Julian. It would seem that her work was not well circulated in her day or in ours. Why is this? I would venture two guesses: First, because she is a woman; and secondly, because she is creation-centered. While Hilton's claim to fame was the tired image of climbing the spiritual ladder, Julian ignores such bouquets to established powers for a way of living that is non-competitive, non-compulsive, that is curved and compassionate to all creatures. In this brief preface I would like to underscore a few of the contributions of Julian to our spiritual needs today. It may well be that another reason she has been so often ignored is that until today we really were not ready for her. This may indeed be the case with many of the great creation-centered mystics such as Hildegarde of Bingen and Meister Eckhart from whom Julian learned so much.

1. **The Creator's and the creation's goodness.** For Julian, the basis of God is not that God is "isness" as Aquinas and Eckhart had taught but that "God is goodness. . .God is nothing but goodness." God's goodness "is full and complete and in it is nothing lacking." But Julian, like Eckhart, goes further. Eckhart had said that not only is "God isness" but that "isness is God." So too with Julian: "God is everything which is good, as I see it, and the goodness which everything has is God." Here we have a metaphysical accomplishment of the first order on Julian's part. For what philosopher in the past few centuries and who in our century of despair and nihilism and holocausts multiplied has the depth and bigness of vision to believe so deeply in the goodness of the source of all things? "That goodness which is natural is God," Julian declares, "God is the ground" of all goodness.

But Julian's metaphysics of goodness does not stop with her understanding of the Creator. What is creation? It is good. "Everything is good except

11

sin, and nothing is evil except sin," Julian declares. Hers is not an introverted spirituality seeking to clean up a bad conscience. Rather, she turns outwards as well as inwards and finds goodness everywhere. "I know well that heaven and earth and all creation are great, generous and beautiful and good." She marvels at the beauty of that portion of creation which is humanity when she sings of "our noble and excellent making." And she overflows with gratitude at the abundance with which the Creator has blessed all creation. "God's goodness fills all God's creatures and all God's blessed works full and endlessly overflows in them." Even God is "delighting without end" at the goodness and beauty of humanity which is "as beautiful, as good, as precious a creature as God could make."

Clearly, Julian does not advise running from creation to experience the divine. For good reason it has been said that her teaching that "the realm of creation is the natural milieu of the Spirit (makes) a radical break with Neoplatonic mysticism."[1]

2. The spirituality of our sensuality. Consistent with her theology of the goodness of creation, Julian does not create body/soul as dualistic or antagonistic. In fact, she does just the opposite: She praises our sensuality and its unique relationship to God. Body and soul form a "glorious union"—how differently Christian theologies of marriage and sexuality would read today had we followed Julian's insights on this topic instead of those of Augustine, who wrote: "The soul makes war with the body." Like Freud, Julian traces our sensuality to our very origins: "It is when our soul is breathed into our body that we are made sensual." Body and soul are to make peace, "let each of them take help from the other," she advises. It is through our sensuality that we receive divine gifts for "God is in our sensuality." Our sensuality "is founded on nature, in mercy and in grace."

But Julian goes even further. She begins to question the use of the word "soul" as it has come to be used in western theology, as if it were a substance apart from our bodiliness. "As regards our sensuality, it can rightly be called our soul because of the union it has with God." One can hardly get any more incarnational than that in one's spirituality! Furthermore, the Creator is the very "glue" that binds our whole self together. "God is the mean which keeps the substance and the sensuality together, so that they will never separate." Here surely is a holiness of wholeness, a quest for healing and one-ing.

3. Salvation as healing. The purpose of the Incarnation for Julian is not so much to scrub away an original sin as to heal the two sides to our nature. Just as in Christ two natures are united—the divine and the

human—so too are we to become whole and healed. By Christ's passion our sensuality is united to our substance by a great act of "oneing." Julian envisions Jesus sitting in our center which is "an honourable city" and which "is our sensuality." Christ is enclosed there. "In our first making God gave us as much good and as great good as we could receive in our spirit alone." Thus for Julian there were two creations: The First which was good, indeed very good; and the second which was Christ's coming as a New Creation which made us even better because it led to a fuller union between the divine and the sensual in us.

The on-going creative power of God is so much a part of us and of creation that all natural activities, including even going to the bathroom, involve us and God working together. "It is God who does this" she declares about going to the bathroom, meaning, it is God and *us*, co-creators that we are. What a far cry from the sentimental prudery of so much Christian spirituality is Julian's investment in our earthliness and in the Good News of Salvation as being the healing news of mind and body, soul and spirit, nature and grace, in unitive acts of peaceful, flowing grace.

4. The Motherhood of God. Julian is rightly famous in our time for her development of the theme of the motherhood of God, a theme that has been so conspicuously absent in the patriarchal spiritualities that have dominated the West in the past few centuries. While this theme is by no means original in Julian—it is present in the Hebrew Bible, in the New Testament, in numerous medieval thinkers like Anselm, St. Francis of Assissi, Mechtild of Magdeburg and Meister Eckhart—still, no one has developed this theme more deeply or more broadly than has Julian of Norwich. Julian ascribes motherhood to God, to the Trinity, to Christ and to the Church. She says, for example, that "in our making, God almighty is our loving Father and God all wisdom is our living Mother." We were created "by the motherhood of love, a mother's love which never leaves us," she declares.

Julian refers to the Trinity as Mother when she says that "the deep wisdom of the Trinity is our Mother, in whom we are enclosed" and that "the property of motherhood" is found in the Trinity. The most prominent and most developed theology of motherhood is found in Julian's treatment of Jesus Christ. Though there is a long tradition in medieval literature on this topic, no one develops it as fully as Julian. "Our Saviour is our true Mother, in whom we are endlessly born and from whom we shall never part." The second person of the Trinity "is our Mother" who by taking on our humanity "has now become our mother sensually. Who is our true mother? "Jesus Christ, who opposes good to evil, is our true

13

Mother. We have our being from him, where the foundation of motherhood begins." Jesus' motherhood applies to both creations, the first and the second. "Jesus is our true Mother in nature by our first creation, and our true Mother in grace by his taking our created nature."

After so many centuries of exclusively patriarchal images for God we are tempted to celebrate Julian's recovery of motherly God images and let it go at that. But this is not enough and it fails to do justice to Julian's considerable intellectual contribution to the theology of the motherhood of God. What in fact does Julian mean by motherhood? And what light does this shed on our spiritual struggles today? Julian identifies the following divine characteristics of motherhood:

• Our experiences of motherhood are our experiences of "being enclosed" according to Julian. Julian is rich in her images of panentheism which she understands as maternal—an enveloping, embracing, welcoming, inclusive, cosmic, expansive, curved image of how we are in God and God is in us. We have here, and in Julian's rich images for these forms, a circular and non-ladderlike, non-competitive image for us, God and society.

• Motherhood reflects the compassionate side of God for Julian, one of 'tender love.' But Julian resists fiercely any sentimentalizing of this motherly love when she insists it is service-oriented. "The mother's service is nearest, readiest and surest," she declares. We are to consider "motherhood at work," she says, if we are to grasp the motherhood of God.

• The work of motherhood includes birthing, with all the pain and struggle that birthing invariably involves. Pain, risk, courage are part of the motherly side of divinity. "We know that all our mothers bear us for pain and for death," she says, and she considers Jesus to be an outstanding example of such divine motherly birthing. The cross is integral to the work of birthing and mothering.

• What is it God gives birth to? God, says Julian, "is the true Father and the true Mother of natures." Thus all beings are birthed by God and "flow out of God to do God's will." Creation itself is the primary birthing activity of the Creator. The relationship of divine motherhood to humans is necessarily a sensual one, according to Julian.

• God is mother insofar as God is "All Wisdom." Drawing on the rich imagery especially of the wisdom tradition of the Hebrew Bible, Julian develops the theme of God as mother, God as wisdom. A patriarchal society defines education exclusively as knowledge. A holistic one would return to education as the quest for wisdom as much as the development of knowledge and information.

5. Humanity's divinization. Another theme that Julian dares to develop is that rich theme in creation-centered spirituality of humankind's divinization. While Eastern Christianity never lost this theme in its theology, the West struggled to keep it alive after the all-pervading influence of Augustine's guilty conscience reduced salvation to cleansing from sin instead of awakening to divine potential, divine beauty. The tradition of our divinization is well attested to in wisdom literature, in the theme so underdeveloped in the West about our being images of God, and in John and Paul. Yet even in our time translators of Julian have made efforts to "clean up" her references to our divinzation. In fact, the theme is altogether orthodox, and when it is lost, spirituality often gets reduced to boring religious pronouncements and sterile legalisms. The reader of Julian would do well indeed to keep this in mind and heart while reading, discussing and praying her meditations in this book. Ponder, for example, these words: "We are of God. That is what we are. I saw no difference between God and our Substance but as if it were all God." Notice, however, that Julian never confuses our divinity with pantheism but has a well-developed and nuanced grasp of panentheism. For continuing on in the phrase I have quoted from she says: "I take this to mean that our substance is *in* God: that is, God is God, and our substance is a creature in God."

6. Other themes. There is a rich treasure house in Julian of all the themes of creation-centered spirituality for the alert reader and pray-er. Not only the five I have alluded to but also the themes of Original Blessing (no creation-centered theologian makes a big thing of original sin). Julian says: "I saw that God never began to love us for. . .we have always been in God's foreknowledge, known and loved from without beginning." Be alert to themes of gratitude, thanksgiving, praise. Of dialectical (both/and) as distinct from dualistic (either/or) images and ways of thinking. Of humor and laughter. Of realized eschatology. Of joy and resurrection, of a mysticism of the empty tomb. Of universal salvation. Of a keen penetration of sin and evil without there being an exaggeration of either's importance. Of church as people, the New Temple, of the mystical body. Of trust and not fear or guilt as the basis of a psychology of spirituality. Of a vulnerable God who suffers and who celebrates.

Julian is a mystic and for our times a prophet who brings us the Good but challenging News of creation-centered theology. Her intellectual and mystical contribution to our lives is untold if we take the time and space to meditate with her, to share and be touched. I can guarantee that it will be time well spent, a time beyond time.

As Brendan Doyle points out in his introduction, every translation is ideological and in fact political. It is therefore especially wonderful to welcome this translation by Brendan Doyle which is born of a deep and mature familiarity with the non-dualistic, creation-centered spiritual tradition from which Julian springs. Thank you too to Patricia Vinje for her considered reflections and concern for Julian and her message that emerges from her foreword.

Matthew Fox, op
Institute in Culture and Creation Spirituality
Holy Names College, Oakland
Oakland, California

---

[1]Brent Pelphrey, "Review of Julian of Norwich, *Showings, 14th Century English Mystics Newsletter*" (September, 1978), p. 28.

PREFACE: Julian's Prophetic Consciousness

"WE were all created at the same time," says Julian of Norwich, "and in our creation we were knit and oned to God." Furthermore, she adds, "God never began to love us...we have always been...known and loved from without beginning."

This cosmic perspective of a woman of the fourteenth century could almost be grasped as a commentary on the first three words of *Genesis*. There the Hebrew words are "br'shyth br' 'lhym," so familiarly translated as "In the beginning God Created." The first word "br'shyth" is a combination of the preposition ("b") "in" or "with" and the word "r'sh" meaning the head of the body. This word is used to express the sum total arrived at by head count and in the book of *Numbers* the same word is used for the counting of the community of Israel by Moses and Aaron. The second "br'," create, is related to the words for blessing, choose, pure, child, and beloved—all images that are suggested by the word creation. The parallel use of the roots "br' " in the first two words of *Genesis* seems to underline the act of creation with a faith that is both poignant and poetic. The word "'sh" within the first word of *Genesis* happens also to be the word for fire or flame—another powerful image that beckons our imagination. Thus in the opening three words of *Genesis* are found the following words: With/everyone/flame/created (blessed, chosen, beloved, pure, child)/God ('lhym). Given this context for *Genesis* 1.1, Julian's statement takes on even greater significance: "We were all created at the same time and in our creation we were knit and oned to God...God never began to love us...we have always been...known and loved from the beginning."

The preposition "with" is further echoed in Julian by her belief that "between God and our soul...there is no between." To believe in *between* is to believe in a separation, a subject/object dualism. The Middle Ages were ruled by Augustine's dictum that we are all under the power of the devil by virtue of original (the "beginning") sin. Original sin destroyed our relationship with God—the beginning of *between*, you might say. With her constant emphasis on "oneing" and "compassion" Julian transcends this dictum with a rich theology of original blessing. In doing so she appears to be in league with the other artists and poets of her age, giving the lie to any accusation that an anchoress could not be in touch with her own culture and respond to it like the prophet that she was. This was the age of wandering minstrels and poets who created the legends that are still alive today, particularly those of the Grail, Percival and Tristan and Isolde. Julian's images are images found in these tales— "longing, "desire," "thirst," "compassion," "sensuality." Her understanding of love as being oned has much in common with them. The legend of Percival, who reunites the sacred lance with the Grail, speaks to us as Julian does with its call to wholeness and liberation. This wholeness and liberation applies to all of nature, for Julian says: "The sky, the earth, failed at the time of Christ's dying because he too was part of Nature." Like Percival, Julian had a cosmic sense. This whole artistic and mystical tradition found another voice in the nineteenth century with Richard Wagner, who created music dramas from these legends. When Julian tells us that our uneasiness is due to finding rest where there is no rest she also seems to echo the same eternal truth so well articulated by the Buddha, another major influence on Wagner.

But Julian's prophetic consciousness goes even further than being in touch with the art of her age. She also turns the tables on the art of courtly love. Much of her language is the language of courtly love, God's "courtesy" (courtliness) probably being the best example. The virtues of courtesy, largesse (hospitality and generosity), truth (fidelity, loyalty) were virtues sought for and respected by chivalrous knights of medieval times. But Julian was a woman. She was not the object of love, not an unattainable married woman lusted after from a distance by some knight—the femme fatale who enjoyed her unattainable status. Instead Julian writes of her love and passion for a God whom she saw as a lord reigning in his castle entertaining his guests. Her love and passion is for a man who showed himself in the pain and graphic wounds of a crucified liberator who was one of and one with us. In courtly love a man of low estate loved from afar a married woman of higher social class. Julian, an anchoress vowed to poverty, sings of her love, longing and desire that will find fulfillment for the God of Might, Wisdom and Love, with the emphasis on Love. Her lover God in turn accepts her love, thirsts for it and enjoys it. Hence Julian's discourse on the true meaning of love is a counterpoint and a redefinion of the virtues so sought after by her male contemporaries—a truly prophetic contribution.

In the *Showings* Julian spends quite a bit of time on Sensuality. Her erotic images of seeing, feeling, hearing, drinking and breathing in God betray a profound and healthy respect for the body—not to mention her wonder at the ordinary and humblest needs of the body which she considers holy. We cannot know God until we know our own soul, and the soul is both Substance and Sensuality. Sensuality, of course, is the miracle of the Incarnation through which we are oned to the Trinity. The body must be kept healthy and strong, and one of the great feats of Compassion is the sorrow experienced on seeing a loved one's body in pain. No masochistic asceticism here. We must remember that Julian's age was also the age of the Black Death, and this experience must have been a vivid one, an awakening to a respect for bodily health.

The Black Death also may have been responsible for Julian's discourse on Motherhood. Barbara Tuchman in her book on the fourteenth century, *A Distant Mirror*, tells us that "women appear rarely as Mothers" in the art of Julian's time. Even the Virgin Mary is portrayed with the child Jesus always at a distance. No attempt was made to illustrate a close relationship. Ms. Tuchman's explanation for this is tied to the fact that the survival rate for children was one out of three. Therefore mothers were afraid to become too close to their children to spare themselves the agony of almost certain separation. Is Julian also trying to redeem the word "mother"? We could say that Julian must have had a wonderful childhood and that she also must have had a very special mother. Another prophetic counterpoint to the culture of Julian's time.

Julian in her stress on the positive, creative and transformative experiences in life does not avoid a healthy acceptance of the Via Negativa. We have already mentioned her Buddhist attitude towards finding rest in material things since God is the True Rest. She also recognizes and speaks of sin. I find it interesting that she sees sin, a failure of our true capabilities, know-how and love, as stemming from sloth and losing of time. Sloth (contrary to a Calvinistic interpretation) was understood in the Middle Ages as a symptom of depression or melancholy leading to despair (what Julian calls "fearful awe"). Julian does not treat sin, therefore, naively. It is a necessary part of life. We are not basically sinful but are basically good, and through sin we grow. This psychology has not lost its freshness and relevance to our own time. We have much to learn from her acknowledgement of the harm caused by guilt and the privatizing of failings so natural to the human condition. Julian says: "Do not accuse yourself too much, allowing your tribulation and woe to seem all your fault; for it is not my will that you be heavy or sorrowful imprudently."

Julian often uses the phrases "in my understanding I saw" and "in my reason I saw." Most of the *Showings* refers to the understanding. I think Julian here means "in my imagination." In our left-brain culture the word imagination (like the word romantic—and Julian was a romantic in the true sense) has taken on pejorative connotations. Gregory Baum has told us that "faith resides in the Imagination." I would add here that the faith of a mystic especially resides in the imagination. Gustav Mahler, the great composer, wrote in one of his letters: "What is it, after all, that thinks within us? And what acts within us? Strange—when I hear music, even while I conduct, I can hear quite clearly that there are no questions at all." "There are no questions at all." What is this if not a firm faith or trust in an intuition received through the imagination? Julian had the same experience I am sure. The vivid paintings of "red, hot blood flowing" through the medium of an imagination stirred through compassion for a human being in pain led to the numerous connections with our own life that we read and call *Showings*—a true work of art. "Reason is the highest gift we have," but our understanding, our imagination is also a gift. Any artists would agree. The experience of artistic creation is a both/and experience.

Julian's answers to all her questions through her imagination sometimes contradicted what she had been taught by "Holy Church" and "clerics." But where her imagination was blessed with an intuition, she believed it, trusted it and let go of images she knew not to be true. Anyone who reads *Showings* can experience the struggle Julian went through between her intuitions and her religious education. Sometimes she goes on for pages trying to justify her religious upbringing, but to no avail. But she does tell us that "Holy Church is *God's* Holy Church," a statement I find very revealing in this context.

A few words now about the language of Julian, especially to those of us who claim English as our mother tongue. In translating certain of Julian's words I found myself being constantly amazed at 1) how so many English words have either lost their meaning today or have taken on a new meaning, 2) the fact that certain translations give truth to the dictum "every translation is an interpretation." Translating words such as "assethmaking" as atonement (as has been done) completely misunderstands and contradicts Julian's emphasis on our blamelessness and the necessity of sin. Asseth-making means making an assessment, i.e., an evaluation, and we have been evaluated as good (Cf. *Genesis* 1), as blessing. Just as Julian tried to redeem words such as "Motherhood" and "Love," I try to save words that have fallen into the hands of a fall/redemption outlook on life. When Julian says we must "empty ourselves of all that is created," she is not saying "we must despise creation", which some translators would have us believe. (The word she uses is, "nowtyn.") In true Eckhartian fashion Julian is telling us to let go of between, to wake up and see that God is in all. Julian's use of the word "comfort" I have translated as "energize" since in medieval England comfort means to give strength to you; when she says "gentle" she is speaking of a relationship, a familial relationship, "of the same *gens*"; "kind," of course, means "nature" and "sensuality" is "sensuality" not *sense soul*. The interpretation I offer in my translation is based on the creation-centered spiritual tradition of which Julian is so rich a part and of which many of her translators have had hardly an inkling.

Brendan Doyle
Institute in Culture and Creation Spirituality
Oakland, California

Since I was only thirty and a half years old, it pained me to think of dying — not because I had special plans for my life nor for fear of any pain.

But I longed to live to love God better and longer here, so I might know and love God more in the joy of heaven.

In so short a time I have experienced so little of life.

I thought my life as nothing and no longer giving praise to the Good Lord.

24

I saw that God is everything that is good
and energizing.

God is our clothing
that wraps, clasps and encloses us
so as to never leave us.

God showed me in my palm
a little thing round as a ball
about the size of a hazelnut.
I looked at it with the eye of my
understanding and asked myself:
"What is this thing?"

And I was answered: "It is everything that
is created."

I wondered how it could survive since
it seemed so little it could suddenly
disintegrate into nothing.

The answer came: "It endures and ever will
endure, because God loves it."

And so everything has being
because of God's love.

Until I am really and truly oned and
fastened to God so that there is nothing
created between us, I will never have
full rest or complete happiness.

For in order to love and have God who is
uncreated, we must have knowledge of the
smallness of creatures and empty ourselves
of all that is created.

We seek rest where there is no rest
and therefore are uneasy.

God is the True Rest
who wants to be known.
God finds pleasure
in being our true resting place.

In our lack of understanding and knowledge
of Love,
We make many intentions when we pray.
But the Goodness of God is the highest
prayer.

God's Goodness kindles our soul and brings
it to life and makes it grow in grace and capacity.

It is closest in nature and most understood
in grace because it is the same grace the
soul seeks and ever shall seek until we
know truly that

we have all been enclosed within God.

Food is shut in within our bodies as in a very beautiful
purse. When necessity calls,
the purse opens and then shuts
again, in the most fitting way. And it is
God who does this

because I was shown that the Goodness of
God permeates us ever in our humblest
needs.

God does not despise creation, nor does
God disdain to serve us in the simplest
function that belongs to our bodies in
nature

because God loves the soul
and the soul is made
in the image of God.

As the body is clothed in cloth
and the muscles in the skin
and the bones in the muscles
and the heart in the chest,

so are we, body and soul,
clothed in the Goodness of God
and enclosed.

For that our soul cleave with all its power
is the one desire of our Lover.

There is no creature that is made
that can know how much
and how sweetly
and how tenderly
our Creator
loves us.

We have the power to ask of our Lover
reverently
all that we desire.

For our natural desire is to have God
and the good desire of God is to have us.

We can never stop this desire or longing
until we have our Lover
in the fullness of joy.

Then can we no more desire.

God
is
everything that is good

and the goodness
that everything possesses
is
God.

Those who have
universal love
for all their fellow Christians
in God
have love towards everything that exists.

For in us all
is comprehended all,

that is,
all that is created
and the Creator of all.

Thus
I saw God
and sought God.

I had God
and failed to have God.

And this is,
and should be,
what life is all about,
as I see it.

God wants us
to allow ourselves
to see God continually.

For God wants
to be seen
and wants
to be sought.

God wants
to be awaited
and wants
to be trusted.

To seek
is as good as
seeing.

God wants us
to search earnestly
and with perseverance,
without sloth
and worthless sorrow.

We must know
that God will appear suddenly
and joyfully
to all lovers of God.

In my understanding
I saw God
in a point.

In seeing this
I saw that God is in all things.

God works in creatures
because
God is in the mid-point of everything
and does all that is done.

But I was sure
that God is not responsible for sin,
because I saw

that sin is no deed.

We perceive
some doings as good
and some as evil,

but our Lord
does not perceive them so.

For just as everything that exists
in nature
is created by God,

so also is everything that is done
God's own doing.

There is no doer but God.

"See!
I am God.
See!
I am in everything.
See!
I do everything.
See!
I never lift my hands off my works,
nor will I ever.
See!
I lead everything
toward the purpose I ordained it to
from without beginning,
By the same Power, Wisdom and Love
by which I created it.

How could anything be amiss?"

My understanding found itself in Heaven
where I saw Our Lord
as a lord in his own house
who had called all his friends
to a formal banquet.

But
I saw that the lord
took no seat in the house.

Instead he reigned as befit a king,
filling the house with joy and glee,
endlessly gladdening and amusing
friends
with kindness, courtesy and
a marvelous melody of endless love.

Every soul
who has willingly served God
in any degree
on earth

shall possess three degrees of happiness
in Heaven.

First,
our Lord will honor and thank them.

Second,
all the creatures in Heaven
will see this honor and thanks.

Third,
this will last forever.

It is God's will
that we do all in our power
to keep ourselves strong
for happiness is everlasting
and pain is passing and will end.

Therefore
it is not God's will
that we pine and mourn
over feelings of pain

but that we get better
and continue to enjoy
life.

Of all pains that lead to liberation
the worst is to see
your loved one suffer.

How could any pain be more excruciating
than to see the one who is
all my life,
all my happiness
and all my joy
suffer?

The greater, the more able and the sweeter
the love is,
the more grief it is to the lover
to see the body of the loved one
in pain.

I saw a great oneing
between Christ and us
because when he was in pain
we were in pain.

All creatures of God's creation
that can suffer pain
suffered with him.

The sky and the earth failed
at the time of Christ's dying
because he too was part of nature.

Thus those who were his friends
suffered pain
because they loved him.

God assigns no blame
to the grumblings and curses
made by the flesh in pain
without the consent of the soul.

The soul,
that noble and joyful life
that is all peace and love,
draws the flesh to give its consent
by grace

And both shall be oned
in eternal happiness.

When someone loves
another creature
in a special way
above all other creatures,

that someone wants
to make all other creatures
love
and find pleasure
in that creature loved so greatly.

Our Lord Jesus oftentimes said:

"This I am.
This I am.
I am what you love.
I am what you enjoy.
I am what you serve.
I am what you long for.
I am what you desire.
I am what you intend.

I am all that is."

God said:

"It is necessary
            that sin should exist.

But
        all will be well,
        and all will be well

        and every manner of thing
            will be well."

I did not see sin:

for I believe
that it has no kind of substance
nor any part of being

nor could it be known
except by the pain it causes.

And this pain purges us
and makes us know ourselves
and to ask compassion.

It would be contrary to nature
to put blame on God
or show any lack of trust
because of *my* sin

since
God does not blame me.

On each person of empty affection
and vicious pride
whom Christ loves

for their own good
he lays something
that is no blame in his sight
by which they are laughed at
and despised in this world,
scorned, taken by force and outcasted.

After that
he will gather them
and make them mild and gentle,
clean and whole

by oneing them to himself.

It is proper to the royal lordship
of God
to have a privy council free from
disturbance.
And it is proper
that those who serve God do not pry
into this council
out of obedience and reverence.
Our Lord understands
and has compassion on those of us
who make themselves so busy trying
to pry into what is none of our business.
I am sure that if we knew how pleasing
it would be to God,
not to mention how much easier
it would be on ourselves,
we would let go of this nosiness.
Even the Saints in Heaven have no desire
to know what God does not want them
to know.
We ought to be like them
since we are all one in God's sight.
We must trust
and be glad for everything.

Our good Lord answered all my questions
and doubts by saying with full energy:

"I can make all things well,
I know how to make all things well,
I desire to make all things well,
I will make all things well.
And you will see with your own eyes
that every kind of thing will be well."

I understand "I can" as referring to
the Father;
"I know how to" to the Son;
"I desire to" refers to the Spirit.
And where God says "I will"
I understand the unity of the Trinity.
"You will see with your own eyes" refers
to the oneing within the Trinity
of all persons who will be liberated.
God wants us to be enclosed in these
words restfully and peacefully.

The spiritual thirst of Christ
is
a love-longing
that lasts and always will
until we are all
together whole in him.

For we are not now
as fully whole
in Christ
as we will be
one day.

Just as there is a property in God
of compassion and understanding,
so also is there a property
of thirst and longing.

This will cease at the end of time
but God's wisdom and love
will not permit
the end to come
until the best time.

We see so much evil around us,
so much harm done,
that we think it impossible
that there is any good in this world.

We look at this in sorrow
and mourn so
that we cannot see God as we should.

This is because we use our reason
so blindly, so unfully
and so simplemindedly
that we are unable to know
the marvelous wisdom, capability
and goodness
of the joyful Trinity.

Just as the joyful Trinity
created all things
out of nothing,

so also this same blessed Trinity
will make well
all that is not well.

"That which is impossible for you
    is not impossible to me:
I will preserve my word in all things
    and I will make all things well."

This is the Great Deed
that Our Lord will do.

Our faith is grounded in God's word
and we must let this faith be.
How it will be done
we will not know until it is done
because God wants us to be at ease
and at peace
not troubled or kept from
enjoying God.

I had a desire to see
Hell and Purgatory—
not to have proof that they exist
but rather to learn everything
I had been taught in my faith
so that my life might profit
from this experience.

But for all my desire
I did not see them.

I understood this to mean
that God and all the holy ones
no more talk about them
than they do about the devil.

The more we busy ourselves
to know God's secrets,
the further away from knowledge
we shall be.

Holy Church is God's Church —

God is the ground,
the substance,
the teaching,
the teacher,
the purpose,
and the reward
for which every soul labors.

The fullness of joy
is
to behold
God
in
everything.

Justice is
that thing that is so good
that it cannot be better
than it is.

For God is Justice.

God creates Justice
in all who will be liberated
through goodness.

God wants
to be known
and loved
through Justice and Compassion
now
and forever.

My own sin
will not hinder the working
of God's goodness.

As long as we are in this life
and find ourselves foolishly
dwelling on sinfulness,
our God tenderly touches us
and joyfully calls us saying:

"Let all your love be, my child.
Turn to me.
I am everything you need.
Enjoy me
and your liberation."

63

God does not want
us to be burdened
because of sorrows and tempests
that happen in our lives,

because
it has always been so
before miracles happen.

God showed me
that I will have to sin.
And I was not too happy
about this revelation.
But I was given the grace to accept it.

But I made the mistake
of privatizing this showing
instead of taking it to mean
my fellow Christians better

What could make me love
my fellow Christian better
than to see that God loves us all
as we were all one soul?

In every soul that will be liberated
is a Godly desire
that never says yes to sin,
nor ever shall.

God showed me
that we should not feel guilty
because of sin
for sin is valuable.

Just as truth answers every sin
by pain,
so also is happiness given to the soul
by love.
Just as different sins are punished
with different pains
according to their seriousness,
so also will these same sins
be rewarded with different joys
in heaven
according to the amount of pain
and sorrow they have caused the soul
on earth.

For we are all precious to God
and God would never have us come there
without rewarding us for our failing.

Peace and love are always in us,
being and working;
but we are not always in peace and love.

God is ground of our whole life in love
and wants us to know this.
God is also our everlasting keeper
and wants us to know this.
God is our friend who keeps us tenderly
while we are in sin
and touches us privately,
showing us where we went wrong
by the sweet light of compassion
and grace,
even though we imagine that we will be
punished.

Often
our trust is not full.

We are not certain
that God hears us
because we consider ourselves
worthless and as nothing.

This is ridiculous
and the cause of our weakness.

I have felt this way myself.

"I am ground of your prayers.

First
it is my will that you have
what you desire,

Later, I cause you to want it.

Later on,
I cause you to pray for it
and you do so.

How then can you not have
what you desire?"

Thanking is
a true understanding of
who we really are.

With reverence and awe
we turn ourselves around
towards the working
that our good Lord incites us
to do,
enjoying and thanking
with our real selves.

True thanking is
to enjoy God.

The fruit
and the purpose
of prayer
is
to be oned with
and like
God
in all things.

It is the will of the Lord
that our prayer and our trust
be large.

We must truly know
that our Lord is the ground
from which our prayer sprouts
and that it is a gift
given out of love,

otherwise
we waste our time
and pain ourselves.

When we think that our prayers
have not been answered
we should not become depressed
over it.

I am certain
that God is telling us
that we must wait for a better time,
more grace,
or that a better gift will be given us.

God is being
and wants us to sit, dwell and ground
ourself in this knowledge
while at the same time realizing
that we are noble, excellent,
assessed as precious and valuable
and have been given creation
for our enjoyment
because we are loved.

Prayer ones the soul to God.

Although we are always like God
in nature and substance,
having been made whole by grace,
we are often unlike God
in our sinful ways.

Prayer is therefore a witness
to the fact that we want
what God wants
and this strengthens our conscience
and empowers us with grace.

Fidelity sees God
and Wisdom keeps God close by
and from these two comes Love—
a delight in God
completely steeped in wonder.

God created all three.
Our soul, a creature in God,
possesses all three
and evermore does all three
for this is the purpose
of its creation.

We were made for Love.

We will all enter our Lord,
fully aware of
and fully possessing God.
This will last forever.

We will truly see,
fully feel,
spiritually hear,
delectably breathe in
and sweetly drink
God.

Holy Church taught me
that sinners
are sometimes worthy of blame
and wrath,

but
I could not see these in God
in my showing.

I saw
that our Lord was never wrathful,
nor ever shall be.
God's lucidity and unity
will not allow this.

God is the goodness
that cannot be wrathful.

Our soul is oned to God,
unchangeable goodness,
and therefore
between God and our soul
there is neither wrath nor forgiveness
because

there is no between.

Our soul must perform two duties.
The one is we must reverently wonder
and be surprised;
the other is we must gently
let go and let be
always taking pleasure in God.
Seeing God in this life
cannot be a continuous experience.
We often fail to see God
and then we fall into ourselves
and feel there is something wrong
with us — that we are perverse
and responsible for the entrance of
sin into the world
and all subsequent sins.
These feelings affect us mentally
and physically.
But the Holy Spirit, the endless life
living within us,
makes us peaceful and at ease,
harmonious and flexible.

I saw wrath and vengeance
only on our part.
God forgives that in us.

For wrath is a turning away from
peace and love
and is opposed to them.

It comes from
a failing of power
or of wisdom
or of goodness
on our part.

The ground of compassion is love
and the working of compassion
keeps us in love.
Compassion is a sweet gracious working
in love, mingled with abundant kindness:
for compassion works at taking care of us
and makes all things become good.
Compassion allows us to fail measurably
and in as much as we fail
in so much we fall;
and in so much as we fall
in so much we die;
for we must die if we fail
to see and feel God
who is our life.
Our failing is fearful,
our falling is shameful
and our dying is sorrowful:
but in all this
the sweet eye of kindness and love
never leaves us, nor does
the working of compassion cease.

Compassion
is a kind and gentle property
that belongs to the Motherhood
in tender love.
And grace is a beautiful property
which belongs to the royal Lordship
in the same love.

Compassion protects, increases our sensitivity,
gives life and heals.
Grace rebuilds, rewards,
endlessly disregarding
what we deserve,
spreading widely
and showing the greatly abundant
and generous hospitality
of the royal Lordship
in God's astonishing courtesy
towards us.

I saw
no kind of vengeance in God,
not for a short time
nor for long —

for, as I see it,
if God were vengeful
even for a brief moment
we would never have
life, place or being.

In God is endless friendship,
space, life and being.

I knew by the common teaching
of Holy Church
and by my own feeling
that the blame for our sins
clings to us continually
while we are on this earth.

How amazing it was then
to see our Lord God
showing us no more blame
than if we were as clean and whole
as the Angels in heaven!

There is a treasure in the earth
that is a food tasty and pleasing
to the Lord.

Be a gardener.
Dig and ditch,
toil and sweat,
and turn the earth upside down
and seek the deepness
and water the plants in time.
Continue this labor
and make sweet floods to run
and noble and abundant fruits
to spring.
Take this food and drink
and carry it to God
as your true worship.

God feels great delight
to be our Father
and God feels great delight
to be our Mother
and God feels great delight
to be our true Spouse
and our soul the loved Wife.

Christ feels great delight
that He is our Brother
and Jesus feels great delight
that He is our Liberator.

These are five great joys
that God wants us to enjoy.

Sometimes we experience such darkness
that we lose all our energy.
But our intent in life
is to continue to live in God
and faithfully trust
that we will be shown
compassion and grace.
This is God's own working in us.
Out of the goodness of God
the eye of our understanding
is opened
by which we see,
sometimes more and sometimes less,
according to the ability
we are given
to receive.

The mingling of both well-being
and distress in us
is so astonishing that we can
hardly tell which state we
or our neighbor are in.
That's how astonishing it is!

But the fact is
that it is part of being whole
both to feel God when God wants us to
and to coexist with God
with all our heart, soul and capability
and then to hate and despise
our evil tendencies and all that
might be occasion of sin
both spiritual and bodily.

We stand in this mingling
all our life.

I saw that God
never *began* to love us.

For just as we will be
in everlasting joy
(all God's creation is destined for this)

so also we have *always* been
in God's foreknowledge,
known and loved
from without beginning.

Faith is
nothing else but
a right understanding
of our being —
trusting
and allowing things to be;

A right understanding
that we are in God
and God
whom we do not see
is in us.

We are of God.
That is what we are.
I saw no difference
betweend God and our Substance
but as if it were all God.

And yet my understanding
took this to mean that
our Substance is *in* God:
that is, God is God
and our Substance is
a creature *in* God.

For the all-capable Fidelity
of the Trinity is our Father
for he created us
and keeps us in him.
The deep Wisdom of the Trinity
is our Mother. In her we are
all enclosed.
The high Goodness of the Trinity
is Christ in whom we are all
enclosed and he in us.

In spite of all our feelings
of sorrow or well-being
God wants us to understand
and know by faith
that we are more truly
in heaven
than on earth.

I understood that
our sensuality is grounded
in Nature, in Compassion
and in Grace.
This enables us to receive
gifts that lead to
everlasting life.
For I saw that in our sensuality
God is.
For God is never out of
the soul.

Our soul is trinitarian
like to the
uncreated Trinity.

It is known
and loved
from without beginning
and in its creation
oned to the Creator.

Because of the beautiful oneing
that was made by God
between the body and the soul

it must be
that we will be restored
from double death.

In the same point
that our soul is made sensual,
in the same point is
the City of God established
from without beginning.

God comes into this seat
and never will remove it.

For God is never out of the soul.

God is nearer to us
than our own soul,
because God is the ground
in which our soul stands
and God is the means
whereby our Substance
and our Sensuality
are kept together
so as to never be apart.

Until our soul is in its full powers
we cannot at all be whole.

By this I mean when our Sensuality
is connected to our Substance
we are made whole
through the strength of
Christ's suffering
and the benefits of our own.
This is accomplished
through compassion and grace.

Both our Substance and Sensuality
together may rightly be called
our Soul.
That is because they are both
oned in God.

Our Sensuality is the beautiful City
in which our Lord Jesus sits
and in which He is enclosed.

Our Substance —
of the same nature as Jesus' —
is also enclosed in Him
with the blessed soul of Christ
sitting restfully
in the Godhead.

98

We
    can never know
          God
                until

    we
      first
          know clearly

          our own soul.

When God was knitted to our body
in the Virgin's womb,
God took our Sensuality
and oned it to our Substance.
Thus our Lady is our Mother
in whom we are all enclosed
and in Christ we are born of her.

And Jesus is our true Mother
in whom we are endlessly carried
and out of whom
we will never come.

We were all created
at the same time;
and in our creation
we were knit and oned to God.
By this we are kept as luminous
and noble
as when we were created.
By the force of this precious oneing
we love, seek, praise, thank
and endlessly enjoy
our Creator.

In Jesus
we have the skillful and wise
keeping of our Sensuality
as well as our restoring
and liberation;

for He is our Mother
Brother
and
Liberator.

Our whole life is in three —

we have our Being,
then our Increasing
and finally our Fulfilling.

The first is Nature,
the second Compassion,
and the third Grace.

Just as
God is
truly
our Father,

so also
is God
truly
our Mother.

God said:

"This I am —
the capability and goodness
of the Fatherhood.
This I am —
the wisdom of the Motherhood.
This I am —
the light and the grace
that is all love.
This I am —
the Trinity.
This I am —
the Unity.
I am the sovereign goodness
of all things.
I am what makes you love.
I am what makes you long and desire.
This I am —
the endless fulfilling of all desires."

A mother's service is
nearest,
readiest
and surest.

This office
no one person
has the ability
or knows how to
or ever will do fully
but God alone.

In God's being is Nature:
that is to say that
that Goodness that is Nature
is God.
God is the Ground, the Substance,
the same thing that is Naturehood.
God is the true Father and Mother
of Nature and all natures that
are made to flow out of God
to work the divine will
will be restored and brought again
into God
by the liberation of persons
through the working of grace.

God has set all natures
in some degree in different creatures.
But in us
all natures exist:
in fullness and in strength,
in beauty and in goodness,
in royalty and nobleness,
in all manner of majesty,
of preciousness and value.

Here we can see
that we are indebted to God
for our nature and grace.

Nature and Grace
are in harmony with each other.
For Grace is God
as Nature is God.
God is two in manner of working
and one in love.
Neither Nature nor Grace
works without the other.
They may never be separated.

Nature is all good and beautiful
in itself,
and Grace was sent out
to liberate nature and destroy sin
and bring beautiful nature
once again to the blessed point
from whence it came:
that is, God.

Nature has been evaluated
in the fire of trying experiences
and no flaw or fault
has been found in it.

It is natural for the child
not to despair of the mother's love.
It is natural for the child
not to be overconfident.
It is natural for the child
to love the mother and
each brother and sister.

I understand no higher state in this
life than childhood
with its minimum of capability and skill
unto the time that our gracious Mother
has led us to our Father's joy.

I understood
that
all the blessed children
who come out of God
by Nature
will be returned into God
by Grace.

We must take God's promises
and energy
as much as our capabilities allow.
This is God's will.
We must also take our trials
and dis-eases
as lightly as we can.
For the more lightly we take them
and the less price we set on them,
for love, the less pain we will have
in feeling them
and the more thanks and refreshment
we will have for them.

God wants to be thought of
as our Lover.
I must see myself so bound in love
as if everything that has been done
has been done for me.
That is to say,
the Love of God makes such a unity
in us
that when we see this unity
no one is able to separate oneself
from another.

I saw the Soul
so large as if it were
an endless world
and a joyful kingdom.
And I understood
that it is a beautiful City.
In the midst of that city
sits our Lord Jesus,
God and one of us,
a beautiful person of large stature
clothed as befit his role
as Bishop and King.
And beautifully he sits,
peacefully and restfully,
in the Soul,
his most familiar home
and endless dwelling.

The soul that realizes on earth
that it is the home and kingdom
of our Lord Jesus
is made like him
and oned to him
in rest and peace
by his grace.
This is full pleasing to God
and great profit to us.

God did *not* say:

"You will *not* be tempested.
 "You will *not* labor hard.
  "You will *not* be troubled."

But God *did* say:

"You will *not* be overcome."

Glad and happy and sweet to our souls
is the joyful, loving face of our Lord.
For he always fixes his eyes upon us
who live in love-longing;
and he wants our soul to smile at him
in return for his favors.
Thus, I hope that with his grace
he has led
and evermore shall join
the Outer Face with the Inner Face
and make us all
one with him
and each of us one with another
in true lasting joy
tnat is Jesus.

I was shown three manners
of our Lord's face.
The face of Suffering that
he showed while here in this life,
dying.
Though this face was mournful and
troubled yet it was glad and joyful,
for he is God.
The face of Empathy and Compassion
he shows with the certainty of caring
to all his lovers who let themselves go
to his love.
The Joyful face was shown more than
the other two and continued
the longest
because this face will exist
endlessly.

Our spiritual eye is so blind
and we are so borne down
by the weight of our mortal flesh
and the darkness of sin
that we are not able to see
our Lord's Joyful face
not at all!
Because of this darkness,
allowing and trusting his great love
and keeping providence
is almost impossible.

Some of us believe
that God is All-Power
and can do all,
and that God is All-Wisdom
and knows how to do all.

But that God is All-Love
and wants to do all,
here we restrain ourselves.

And this ignorance hinders
most of God's lovers,
as I see it.

Just as God courteously forgives
our sin after we change our ways,
so also does God want *us*
to forgive *our* sin
instead of falling into
a false meekness
that is really a foul blindness
and weakness due to
fear.

God showed two sorts of sickness
that we have:
The one is our lack of ability
to endure, or sloth —
for we bear our toil and our pains
heavily.
The other is despair,
or fearful awe.
In general God showed *sin*
in which *all sin* is comprehended,
but in special I was shown
only these two.
They are the sins that cause
the most pain and tempest us.

We should desire to regard our Lord
with wondering reverence
rather than fear,
loving God gently and trusting
with all we are capable of.
For when we regard God with awe
and love God gently
our trust is never in vain.
The more we trust,
and the more powerful this trust,
the more we please and praise
our Lord whom we trust in.
Without this,
we cannot please God.

God is thirsty for everyone.

This thirst has already drawn
the Holy to Joy
and we the living
are ever being drawn and drunk.

And yet
God still thirsts and longs.

Not only will we receive
the same joy that souls
previously have had in heaven,
but we will also receive
a new joy
which will be flowing
copiously
out of God
into us
fulfilling us.

God says:

"Do not accuse yourself too much,
allowing your tribulation and woe
to seem all your fault;

for it is not my will
that you be heavy or sorrowful
imprudently."

Our Lord is with us,
taking care of us
and leading us into
the fullness of joy.

Our way
and our heaven
is
faithful love
and sure trust.

I believe and understand
the ministration of angels,
as clerics tell us —

but
it was not shown me.

For God is nearest and gentlest,
highest and lowest,
and does everything —
not only everything we need
but also everything that is
valuable for our joy in heaven.

Astonishing and stately is our soul —
the place where our Lord lives.

Therefore God wants us to respond
whenever we are touched,
rejoicing more in God's complete love
than sorrowing over
our frequent failings.

Love
makes God long for us.
And in this manner of longing
and waiting
God wants us to do the same.
This is our natural penance —
and the highest, as I see it.
For this penance will never
leave us
until we are fulfilled
and possess God to the fullest.
Therefore God wants us
to set our hearts away from
the pain we feel
into the joy
we trust will be ours.

God says:

"I love you,
and you love me,
and our love
will never be divided in two:

for your benefit
I allow sin to fall to you
against your will.

I am taking care of you.

Believe me."

The three properties of God are
Life, Love and Light.
In Life is the astonishing
familiarity of home,
In Love is courtesy as befits
a relationship,
and in Light
is endless Nature-hood.

I saw that our Reason is in God,
and is the highest gift
we have received.
It is grounded in Nature.

Our Faith is a light
naturally coming from
our endless Day, our Father God.
In this light our Mother, Christ,
and our good Lord, the Holy Spirit,
lead us
in this passing life.

The natural light of Faith
has its own separate bounds
but needfully stands to us
in the night.
The light is cause of our life;
the night cause of our pain and woe.
We deserve refreshment and thanks
from God
because we, with compassion and grace
and a firm desire, know and believe
our light, going into it wisely
and as much as we can.
And at the end of our woe,
suddenly our eyes will be opened
and in this translucence
our sight will be full.

It was said to me:

"Do you wish to see clearly
your Lord's meaning
in these Showings?

See it well.

Love
          was your Lord's meaning.

Who showed it to you?
Love.
What did you see?
Love.
Why was it shown?
For Love."

On the last day
we will clearly see in God
the secret counsels
that now are hidden from us.
Then none of us will be stirred
to say:
"Lord, if we would have known
these things,
then all would have been well."

Instead
we will all say with one voice:

"Lord, may you be blessed!
For it is thus:

it *is* well."

Publisher's Note:

Bear & Company is publishing this series of creation-centered mystic/prophets to bring to the attention and prayer of peoples today the power and energy of the holistic mystics of the western tradition. One reason western culture succumbs to boredom and to violence is that we are not being challenged by our religious traditions to be all we can be. This is also the reason that many sincere spiritual seekers go East for their mysticism—because the West is itself out of touch with its deepest spiritual guides. The format Bear & Company has chosen in which to present these holistic mystic/prophets is deliberate: We do not feel that more academically-styled books on our mystics is what every-day believers need. Rather, we wish to get the mystics of personal and social transformation off our dusty shelves and into the hearts and minds and bodies of our people. To do this we choose a format that is ideal for meditation, for imaging, for sharing in groups and in prayer occasions. We rely on primary sources for the texts but we let the author's words and images flow from her or his inner structure to our deep inner selves.